This 1902 Arrol-Johnston is typical of the company's early products. A horizontally opposed flat-twin engine is located under the floor, the driver sits behind the front-seat passengers and the tyres are solid rubber with spoon brakes. This example, photographed in 1946, is still in running order.

THE SCOTTISH
MOTOR INDUSTRY

Michael Worthington-Williams

Shire Publications Ltd

CONTENTS

Introduction 3
Arrol-Johnston, Galloway and
   Arrol-Aster 5
Albion cars and commercials 13
Argyll 17
Other Scottish motor manufacturers . 23
Further reading 32
Places to visit 32

Printed in Great Britain by C. I. Thomas & Sons (Haverfordwest) Ltd, Press Buildings, Merlins Bridge, Haverfordwest, Dyfed SA61 1XF.

British Library Cataloguing in Publication Data: Worthington-Williams, Michael. The Scottish Motor Industry. 1. Scotland. Car Industries. I. Title. 338.4'7629 222' 09411. ISBN 0-7478-0038-3.

Editorial consultant: Michael E. Ware, Curator of the National Motor Museum, Beaulieu.

ACKNOWLEDGEMENTS
I should like to acknowledge the pioneer research carried out by Nick Baldwin, A. S. E. Browning, A. Craig Macdonald BSc, Lytton Jarman, Lord Montagu of Beaulieu, M. Morton Hunter, Duncan Robertson, Neale Lawson, Tom Love and the late Michael Sedgwick, which has materially assisted the author in the preparation of this book.

Cover: *A 15.9 horsepower four-cylinder Arrol-Johnston touring car, from the front cover of their 1925 catalogue.*

Below: *Carnoustie, Angus, was the home of the handsome Dalhousie, built by the Anderson-Grice Company Limited, better known for its foundry equipment and crane building. Designed by A. G. Grice (later designer of GWK cars) and of rakish appearance, the Dalhousie was made in limited numbers until 1910. James Law, an Arbroath motor engineer, purchased all the spares and may have assembled a few more.*

Old-established coachbuilders J. and C. Stirling of Hamilton, Lanarkshire, built their first Stirling-Daimler Stanhope in 1897. It followed Daimler lines, employed a 4 horsepower Daimler engine but carried their own coachwork. The cars were still being assembled in small numbers as late as 1902, by which time the company had moved to Granton, Edinburgh.

INTRODUCTION

Scotsmen, rather than Scotland, figure largely in the history of science and industry, and William Murdoch, who was born in Ayrshire, built one of the earliest road-going self-propelled carriages in 1784. Murdoch's employer, James Watt, born in Greenock, despite his vision in other areas of steam-engine development, had an intense dislike for steam carriages and their sponsors, however, and dissuaded Murdoch from patenting his machine.

If Watt was hostile to road transport, however, his fellow countrymen John Loudon McAdam (1756-1836) and Thomas Telford (1757-1834) more than redressed the balance by the contributions they made to the road systems of both England and Scotland, and this indirectly assisted the development of the 'horseless carriage' in Scotland when it first appeared there more than half a century later.

The story of the Scottish motor industry is mainly the story of three major companies, Arrol-Johnston, Albion and Argyll, but of these only Albion survived into modern times, and they built only commercial vehicles after 1913. Nevertheless, at various times Scotland has supported well over fifty indigenous and independent manufacturers of motor vehicles — cars, commercials and motorcycles — many of which were as good, if not better, than their English, continental and American rivals. That they failed to survive is more a consequence of geography, management and economics than of shortcomings in quality, design or innovation.

The Scottish motor industry never fully recovered from the effects of the First World War, and its story is mainly of slow decline from 1914 onwards. With the exception of the Hillman Imp plant at Linwood (subsequently purchased by Talbot) and the continuing activity of Argyll Turbo Cars Limited at Lochgilphead and Lanark, private car production in Scotland effectively ceased with the final closure of Arrol-Aster's Dumfries factory in 1931. Admittedly Argyll (no connection with the present company) struggled on for a further year, but it is unlikely that it built any new cars after 1927. At its peak in the Edwardian period, however, that company ranked fifth in size and production amongst British motor manufacturers.

The last wholly Scottish-built car was produced as long ago as the 1930s, and today few people are aware of Scotland's motoring heritage and even fewer have ever seen a Scottish car. This book aims to chronicle the activities of those Scottish pioneers, large and small, conventional and iconoclastic and their successes and failures. It is, of necessity, an incomplete narrative as the story is a continuing one. In recent years the Stonefield cross-country truck has been developed by Jim McKelvie at Paisley, and the Terex off-road vehicles are being manufactured by General Motors Scotland at Motherwell. It may be that the Argyll GT signals a revival of the Scottish motor industry.

This 1921 Gilchrist was registered in Ayrshire and carries the badge of the Royal Scottish Automobile Club. A Gilchrist, driven by George Cutbush, editor of 'Motor World', officiated at the Scottish Reliability Trials. Only about twenty were built.

A number of makes of motorcycle were once built in Scotland, and the most successful of these was the Victoria, built by the Victoria Motor and Cycle Company based at Dennistoun, Glasgow. Between 1902 and 1926 they offered a wide range of single-cylinder and twin-cylinder machines of good quality, with engines by Precision, Villiers, JAP and Blackburne. At the top of the range a 688 cc Coventry-Victor flat twin found a few buyers.

4

By 1914 Arrol-Johnston had adopted a radiator-behind-engine layout, and the 'coal-scuttle' type bonnet was reminiscent of that used on Renaults of the same period. This is a 15.9 horsepower model of about 1912.

ARROL-JOHNSTON, GALLOWAY AND ARROL-ASTER

Although it is commonly believed that the first British-built car owing nothing to continental design was the Lanchester of 1896, George Johnston, a locomotive engineer from the works of the Hydepark Locomotive Company Limited of Springburn, Glasgow, conceived his first car as early as 1894 and had probably built it by 1895. The Mo-Car Syndicate Limited of Bluevale, Camlachie, Glasgow, was formed towards the end of 1895 by Johnston, his cousin Norman Osborne Fulton and Thomas Blackwood Murray, with finance provided by Sir William Arrol, the architect of the Forth Bridge and an eminent consulting engineer, to manufacture the Arrol-Johnston car.

The petrol-engined Arrol-Johnston performed well, climbing the one in five gradient of Douglas Street in Glasgow successfully and attaining 17 mph (27 km/h) on the level (for which achievement Johnston was fined 2s 6d). Mechanically the cars were unconventional. A large twin-cylinder underfloor horizontal-

ly opposed engine transmitted power by primary chain to a gearbox which, on later models at least, provided four forward speeds, with single-chain final drive and solid tyres. Dogcart bodywork was fitted, and in the six-seater model the driver sat in the second row. Modern features were a self-locking and tilting steering wheel, which was fitted quite early on, and a rope and pulley operated self-starter.

By 1904 the company had begun to explore the possibilities of the commercial-vehicle market and a 2 ton van with 12 horsepower engine similar to that used in the car was joined in August 1904 by a sixteen-seat charabanc capable of 12 mph (19 km/h). J. S. Napier joined the company as chief engineer in 1905 to update design and an entirely new company, the New Arrol-Johnston Car Company Limited, was formed, with backing from Sir William Beardmore (later Lord Invernairn), who also became company chairman.

Following the unsuccessful 'Victory' model of 1919, Arrol-Johnston quickly resurrected the pre-war 15.9 horsepower type, but with front-mounted conventional radiator and bonnet. This example is fitted with open-drive limousine body and was probably used for private hire.

Napier's initial design, an orthodox 18 horsepower twin, was entered in the 1905 TT (a 'fuel consumption' event) and, driven by its designer, it narrowly beat Percy Northey's Rolls-Royce 20 horsepower to first place at an excellent average speed of 33.9 mph (54.6 km/h). Later competition failures, however, led to withdrawal from racing after 1912.

An overdue move to new premises followed a fire in 1906. Archibald Coats, a member of the original Mo-Car Syndicate, offered his large thread mill at Underwood, Paisley, and production rose to seven hundred units a year by 1907. There were no more TT successes and, following disagreements, Johnston left to form his own company at Bridgeton.

Blackwood Murray and Fulton had already left in 1899 to form Albion and when Johnston departed two large four-cylinder cars with pair-cast cylinders were introduced — the 24/30 (retained for one season only) and the 38/45, both of which were marketed alongside the horizontal-engined 12/15 horsepower twin. An inlet-over-exhaust 16/25 model with dual ignition, designed by Napier, appeared in

1908 and this, together with the 12/15 and the 38/45, covered the 1909 season as well.

A specially designed air-cooled car for use on Ernest Shackleton's Antarctic expedition gained considerable publicity. A four-cylinder engine with separately cast cylinders and overhead inlet valves with Renault-type 'coal scuttle' bonnet, tractor-type wheels, a pick-up body and detachable skis for the front wheels made a thoroughly practical-looking vehicle.

In April 1909 T. C. Pullinger joined the company as general manager, having been previously with Sunbeam and Humber, and his 15.9 horsepower model made its appearance at the 1909 Motor Show. It was a conventional car, with a Renault-style bonnet like the Shackleton vehicle and with the radiator behind the engine.

A 23.8 horsepower six-cylinder model appeared briefly in 1911, but a smaller 11.9 horsepower 'four' was added to the range and the 15.9 horsepower was improved. Dynamo lighting was an option in 1913 and in the same year the company moved to Heathhall, Dumfries. By 1914 the 15.9 horsepower tourer could be had with both electric starting and lighting for

6

a modest £360. The 'six' was followed by a four-cylinder 20.9 horsepower model, but production soon ceased in favour of war work and the manufacture of aero-engines was undertaken at a new factory at Tongland, Kirkcudbright.

Arrol-Johnston was one of the first companies to announce an entirely new post-war model, the 17.9 horsepower Victory. The company had acquired the services of G. W. A. Brown from Clement-Talbot. He was almost as experienced as Pullinger and on paper the Victory looked good, being up-to-date and innovative. Handbrake and gear change were centrally placed in the most modern American manner; the engine had an overhead camshaft; bodywork was streamlined and attractive, and the whole car weighed only a ton. Unfortunately, it was a monumental failure. Rushed into production too quickly in order to catch the post-war orders, it proved unreliable. Moreover, its shortcomings were highlighted when one supplied to the Prince of Wales in August 1919 for a victory tour was ignominiously withdrawn before the itinerary had been completed. The Victory was hurriedly abandoned and the pre-war 15.9 horsepower model was revived — updated with a frontal radiator and reverting to its original bore and stroke — and because of the shortage of cars in 1919 it sold quite well, although basically a ten-year-old design.

Arrol-Johnston badly needed a new model to sell and re-opened the Tongland factory for production of a light car based on the Fiat 501 and named the Galloway. Supervision of the Tongland plant was deputed to Pullinger's daughter Dorothée and it was staffed largely by women, many of whom had worked there during the war. The Victory central-ball change-gear control was used and the thrifty management melted down back-axle casings from that model for the casting of the Galloway engine. The new make proved moderately successful.

About fifty 15.9 horsepower cars were produced at Heathhall each week in 1920. In 1922 unit construction of the engine and gearbox, semi-elliptic springs

The 1921 Galloway 10.5 horsepower model was based on the side-valve engined Fiat 501. Although financed by Arrol-Johnston, it was built in a separate factory erected during the First World War at Tongland, Kirkcudbright. Dorothée Pullinger was in charge (her father was chief engineer at Arrol-Johnston) and the factory was staffed largely by women.

A 1920 Arrol-Johnston 15.9 horsepower model still on the road. Typical of open four- or five-seater tourers of the period, it is fitted with only three doors. The driver's door is a dummy because brake and gear levers mounted on the right of the driver would prevent entry to the vehicle on this side.

By 1923 the Galloway had become a 10.9 horsepower model with a slightly enlarged engine capacity. Withdrawn in 1925, it was replaced by a Twelve with pushrod-operated overhead valves. For its day the Galloway was modern, with engine and gearbox in-unit and central-control gearbox.

8

The Arrol-Johnston works at Heathhall, Dumfries, to which Galloway production was transferred in 1923, was modern, utilitarian and efficient, in stark contrast to Argyll's palatial factory at Alexandria by Glasgow. Arrol-Johnston were quick to capitalise on this, telling customers 'all our money goes into the cars'.

The bodywork of this 1928 Galloway 12/30 fixed-head coupé at Olympia reflects the influence of Aster of Wembley, with which Galloway's parent company, Arrol-Johnston, amalgamated in 1927. It was one of the last, the Galloway disappearing as a separate make at the end of 1928 as a result of rationalisation of the range.

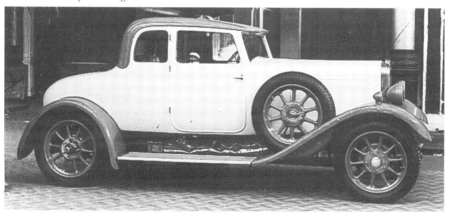

and a monobloc engine with detachable head were introduced. Tongland was closed down and Galloway production was transferred to Heathhall, and in 1924 a 2.1 litre Fourteen and 3.2 litre Colonial model were introduced. The latter had neither front-wheel brakes nor shock absorbers — a fact tartly noted by the press — and the deficiency remained unremedied into 1925. The range then became complicated, the Fourteen giving way to a Twelve, which shared its engine with a Galloway of the same size. The 10

horsepower Galloway was discontinued, as was the 12 horsepower Arrol-Johnston, and the remaining models, acquired overhead valves.

In April 1927 the company amalgamated with Aster of Wembley, Middlesex, proprietary engine makers who had commenced car manufacture in 1922. Aster aimed at the luxury market and at the time of the amalgamation were using a Burt-McCollum single sleeve-valve engine on their largest model, the 23/70 horsepower.

9

New for 1929 was the luxurious straight-eight cylinder Arrol-Aster 23/70, seen here in five-seater tourer form. It was a disastrous year in which to introduce a car costing £798, for in June the American stock market collapsed, precipitating a world depression in trade.

Sir Malcolm Campbell's 1928 Land Speed Record contender, the Napier-engined Arrol-Aster, photographed at Heathhall during construction of the body, possibly late in 1927. The car achieved 206.96 mph (333.06 km/h) at Daytona, Florida, in February 1928 to set a new record. This was beaten two months later by the Triplex Special at 207.55 mph (334.01 km/h).

The range now became even more complicated, with the Galloway, the Arrol-Johnston and the smaller model Arrol-Aster having overhead valves, whilst larger Arrol-Asters and Asters had sleeve valves. The Aster's attractive .bodywork was fitted to all models and the range was simplified in 1928 when all but three models were dropped.

The Galloway now defunct, the company developed a straight-eight sleeve-valve model but, despite a contract to rebuild Sir Malcolm Campbell's *Bluebird* and a revival of sporting interest with supercharged straight eights in the TT and Alpine Trials, the company went into liquidation in 1929. Arrol-Asters were made in small numbers by the liquidators and the company was still nominally in business until 1931.

Showing its Aster ancestry, this 1929 Arrol-Aster 23/70 coachbuilt coupé cost £798 and had one-shot chassis lubrication, Silentbloc bearings on the spring shackles and the then innovative chromium plating.

The 23/70 Arrol-Aster coachbuilt saloon carried extra-large brake drums and comfortably accommodated five people. The two front seats were adjustable; a roller blind on the rear window could be operated from the driver's seat, and other equipment included an automatic screen wiper, ladies' and gentlemen's vanity sets and red leather (or brown furniture hide) interior trim. Cellulose options included black, two shades of blue, brown or grey to the customer's choice.

This 1901 Albion Station Cart with 'dos-à-dos' seating is very typical of the earliest tiller-steered type, with under-floor opposed-piston twin-cylinder engine. Wheel steering came a year later, and in 1903 production of a 16 horsepower vertical twin commenced. This remained available for many years and was popular in shooting-brake form.

A former War Department Albion photographed outside the South London premises of the St George's Motor Company, coachbuilders, before its delivery to Woodford Laundries of Woodford, London. At this period few commercial vehicles carried windscreens.

Former War Department Albion lorries were often re-bodied for civilian use following the Armistice of 1918, and this solid-tyred chain-driven example is typical. It was supplied to J. Bennett, a fishmonger of South Norwood, London, by St George's Motor Company shortly after the vehicle had been released by the War Disposals Board from the vehicle dump at Slough, Berkshire.

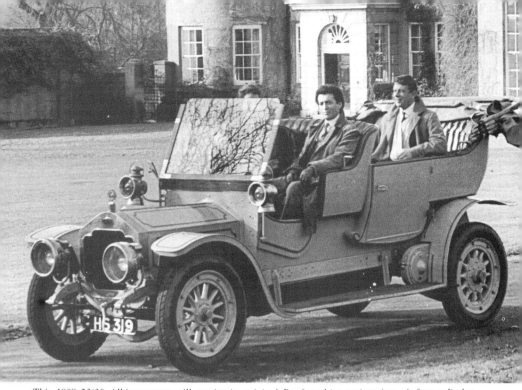

This 1909 23/30 Albion tourer still carries its original Renfrewshire registration. A four-cylinder model, but still retaining chain final drive, it was introduced in 1906 and had a seven-year production run. The side-valve engine was of 5.6 litres capacity.

ALBION CARS AND COMMERCIALS

Thomas Blackwood Murray was born in 1871 at Heavyside and graduated from Edinburgh University at the age of nineteen as a Bachelor of Science in Engineering, taking an early interest in transport. He and Norman Fulton left the Mo-Car Syndicate (headed by the latter's cousin, George Johnston) in 1899 and Fulton went to America to study production methods. Premises were taken at 169 Finnieston Street, Glasgow, and finance came from Thomas's father, John Murray, who mortgaged his farm for the sum of £1500 — little enough upon which to establish the Albion Motor Car Company.

After a year's design work, construction of the first car started early in 1900, and by 1902 nearly sixty cars of 8 and 10 horsepower had left the tiny works. The early cars were influenced by Arrol-Johnston design, engines being of the horizontal type until 1903. Murray,

however, was an innovator, and his patent lubricator, operating to all working parts from the driver's seat, was still in use in improved form during the First World War on ABC Dragonfly aero-engines. The Murray Engine Speed Governor also survived well into the First World War period, and the low-tension ignition system introduced on the Arrol-Johnston came with Murray to Albion.

Albion concentrated on cars with robust dogcart bodywork, building their reputation on solid reliability rather than any outstanding feature of design or performance. In 1901 they did well in the Glasgow Trials and began to build commercial vehicles and to export. In 1903 the company moved to Scotstoun, Glasgow, remaining there until 1972, when production of vehicles bearing the Albion name ceased.

The 1904 Albion range included a 12 horsepower dogcart with vertical front-mounted engine and a commercial 1 ton chassis, whilst in 1905 a solid-tyred 16 horsepower twin was offered, although pneumatics were also available. All Albion bodies were built by Penman of Dumfries. In 1906 the company entered the luxury market with a four-cylinder 24 horsepower model with twin side-chain final drive and this, together with the 16 horsepower, accounted for much of Albion's private-car production.

In 1912 a T-head 15 horsepower model replaced the larger 24 horsepower chauffeur-driven type. With monobloc engine, engine in unit with gearbox and worm-drive, it was a distinct improvement. However, Albion's stand at Olympia in 1913 displayed only shooting brakes. Only 150 private cars left the factory that year, about a quarter of total production, and a 15 horsepower coupé announced in November 1913 was the last true private car made. During the war they built some six thousand of their B-type trucks for the War Department.

One of the first manufacturers to introduce new models after the war, Albion nevertheless continued production of the B-type until 1927, by which time about nine thousand had been made. The 30 cwt (1524 kg) subsidy chassis, however, entered production in 1923 and this remained the basis of all their lighter models well into the next decade.

In 1923 they introduced a 14/16 seater charabanc, the Viking, which combined low lines with good looks and adopted pneumatic tyres, permitting speeds of up to 30 mph (48 km/h) in comfort. A

drop-frame bus (one of the first) followed in 1925 and the Viking was offered with the 30/60 horsepower engine as an option, which increased speed to 40 mph (64 km/h), and from 1929 a six-cylinder engine was available. By then Albion offered a range from 30 cwt (1524 kg) up to 5 tons.

A six-tonner and a very successful 3/4½ ton lightweight appeared in 1931 and a six-cylinder bus, the Valiant, was produced, as well as the twenty-seater Victor. The firm also moved into the double-decker market with the Venturer, which used the same engine as the Valiant. From 1932 diesel options (with engines by Gardner, Dorman or Beardmore) were available on most of the heavier Albions in the range, but from late 1933 their own diesel engine was produced. During the Second World War Albion was a major supplier of four-wheel-drive three-tonners and 6 x 4 ten-tonners, in addition to some thousand tank transporters which achieved 140 horsepower in production form.

In 1951 the company was acquired by Leyland Motors and vast expansion followed, with the adoption of Leyland engines for some models. The 1958 eight-wheeler Albion Caledonian was, however, virtually identical to the Leyland Octopus and other rationalisation inevitably followed, although Albion continued to make its own 5.5 litre engine in the 1960s. By 1969 independent technical development of Albion products was almost at an end and in 1972 the name was phased out.

Albions were popular with coach and bus operators. This forward-drive saloon coach was delivered new to Herbert Richmond of Richmond's Coaches, Epsom, Surrey, around 1930 and was bodied by Warwick Motor Body Works. Note the canvas folding roof.

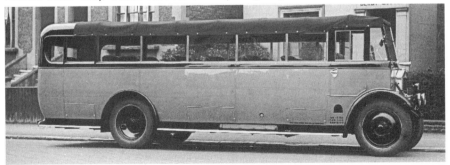

This 30 cwt (1524 kg) Albion van dates from around 1930 and was the smallest commercial in a range which extended up to five-tonners. Delivered new to the Good Shepherd Laundry of Finchley, London, it was coachbuilt by Warwick Motor Body Works of Parson's Mead, West Croydon, Surrey.

Bearing on its radiator Albion's slogan, 'Sure as the sunrise' (and what may be an Arabic translation underneath), this mid 1930s Albion plied the dangerous desert route between Baghdad and Jerusalem and thence to Damascus. Five layers insulate the roof from the heat.

15

This 1902 Argyll would have been made in the Bridgeton premises of the Hozier Engineering Company Limited, before the move to Alexandria. Powered by a 12 horsepower vertical twin engine (both Clement and Aster units were used), it featured Alex Govan's patent gearbox. This example was owned new by Alfred Clarkson of Clapham Park, London.

An original factory photograph of the 16/20 Argyll of about 1905. The car appears to carry no provision for a hood and the windscreen is braced by leather straps to the front dumb irons.

Photographed in the Cardiff area and bearing a Carmarthen registration, this Aster-engined Argyll of about 1905-6 has four- to five-seater side-entrance tonneau bodywork, a windscreen and, unusually, oil headlamps at a time when acetylene was more common.

ARGYLL

In 1899 Alex Govan took over the old premises of the defunct Scottish Cycle Company at Hozier Street, Bridgeton, Glasgow, and designed and built a light car. Finance was provided by W. A. Smith of the National Telephone Company and the Hozier Engineering Company Limited was set up with a capital of £15,000 to manufacture Argyll cars.

Purpose-built, with tubular steel chassis, full elliptic springs and handlebar steering, the car resembled those of Louis Renault. It was powered by a British MMC-built De Dion engine of 258 cc and, like the Renault, used shaft drive rather than chains. With cycle-type wheels, it was altogether lighter and less clumsy looking than its contemporaries in Scotland. The four-speed gearbox was designed by Govan, power being transmitted via an internal leather-lined cone clutch and depression of the clutch pedal also operated the footbrake.

By 1901 a 5 horsepower MMC engine was used and steering-column change had given way to the then more usual side-change speed lever. Wheel steering and a distinctive radiator followed, but Govan's gearbox was difficult to operate and required a separate lever for reverse gear.

The cars performed well in the 1901 Glasgow Trials, and 1902 models had an 8 horsepower Simms engine and Simms-Bosch magneto ignition but an MMC-powered version of the same size was also offered. 10, 12 and 16 horsepower models were available later that year. By April eight cars a week were leaving the works and by January 1904 this had increased to fifteen. 1904 was also the first year in which Argyll offered an engine of their own manufacture — the 12 horsepower — although units by Aster powered their 10 and 16 horsepower models, De Dion made the 8 horsepower engine and Clement engines had also been used.

Honeycomb radiators appeared on all models in 1905, the last year in which the single-cylinder type was made, and an Argyll-engined 20/24 featured dual ignition and a three-speed gearbox of Govan design and claimed a top speed of 60 mph (97 km/h). Argylls proved just as robust as the heavier products of Arrol-Johnston and matched the somewhat agricultural

17

A 16/20 Argyll fitted with what appears to be a town car body in which the passengers are fully enclosed but the driver has no protection whatever. Argyll opened an export department very early and enjoyed considerable popularity overseas. This photograph was taken in the Middle East, probably in Cairo.

specification of the latter with high-speed engines, long piston stroke, coil ignition, pneumatic tyres, live axles and thermo-siphon cooling of the radiator, which obviated the use of a water pump.

In March 1904, driving an Argyll, Douglas Whitehead completed the John O'Groats to Land's End journey in ten hours less than the existing record held by J. W. Stocks. In August of that year E. J. Robertson Grant, also in an Argyll, reduced the record to 42 hours 5 minutes, and Argylls did well in trials in India and Australia as well as Britain.

A van was built on the 10/12 horsepower chassis and a truck department was set up under John Brimlow, previously with Stirling Motor Carriages at Granton, Edinburgh.

Argyll built Aster engines under licence from 1906 and initially the operation was supervised by French engineers. Showroom premises were opened in London, including a motor school which even catered for lady drivers by providing instructresses. They were also ahead of their time in issuing free bi-monthly engineers' reports on customers' cars, a forerunner of the service schemes which most of the larger manufacturers did not introduce until the 1950s.

In March 1905 a new company, Argyll Motors Limited, was formed and a new factory built at Alexandria by Glasgow. It was unlike any motor factory which existed at that time. With its noble porticos, marble halls, palatial lavatories and cloakrooms, test hill and testing track, the whole complex was years ahead of its time. By 26th June 1906 all was ready for a grand opening, two stands were taken at the Olympia Motor Show and Argyll's own house magazine, probably the first of its kind in Europe, became available under the title *The Motorist*. Where Alexandria failed — and it was virtually doomed from the start — was not so much in the lavishness of its

18

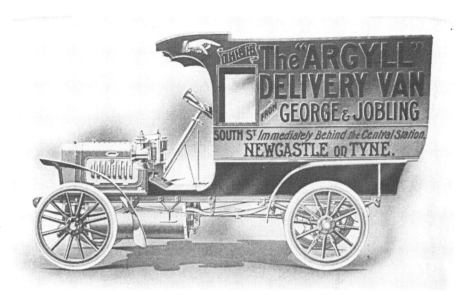

Argyll was early in the field of commercial vehicles, this 10/12 horsepower twin-cylinder delivery van being offered in 1904. Priced at £350 and fitted with 3 inch (76 mm) solid tyres, it shared many features with the Argyll car of the same period.

One of the last of the poppet-valve engined Argylls, a 12/18 tourer of about 1912 fitted with unusual single centre-mounted acetylene headlamp. The generator is on the nearside running board. This car carries a London registration and was probably sold through Argyll's London depot off Oxford Street.

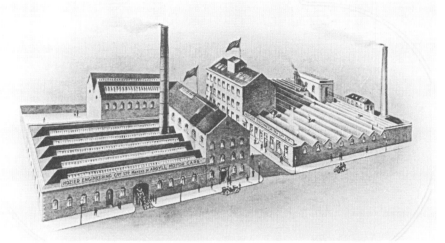

The original Argyll works of the Hozier Engineering Company Limited at Bridgeton, Glasgow, as it looked in 1904. Manufacture of Argyll cars resumed here under John Brimlow's direction in 1920, following the bankruptcy of the Alexandria factory in 1914.

This 1925 12 horsepower Argyll was built at Bridgeton for the 1926 season but was not up to the standards of the earlier cars. Engines and axles were bought in from Greenwood and Batley of Leeds and Wallace (Glasgow) Limited, the tractor makers. The single sleeve-valve principle was adhered to, however, but the firm's last Motor Show appearance was in 1927.

appointments but in the manner of its operation. An enterprise so vast and expensive (£200,000) could be justified only if the level of production rose significantly above that of Bridgeton — indeed, above that of most of Argyll's competitors on both sides of the Atlantic. It never did.

There was nothing wrong with the cars, however: Robertson Grant drove successfully in the Herkomer Trophy Trials and McTaggart broke the existing record for a run from one end of Ireland to the other, although a second place in the TT was marred by disqualification.

In 1907 the company was manufacturing the 10/12, three Aster-engined four-cylinder models and the 14/16 with

Argyll's own unit, as well as a full range of cab-over-engine trucks and taxicabs. In May Alex Govan achieved a non-stop run in the Irish Reliability Trials driving a 12/14 model, but it was to be his last publicity earner for the company and his last service to Argyll, for he contracted ptomaine poisoning and died a week later at the age of 38 — a tragedy from which Argyll never recovered.

Competition successes continued, however, although it seemed that the publicity department was less able to make the most of them. Two new models were announced for 1908: an Aster-engined 12/16 with neat monobloc layout and a large Forty with separately cast cylinders, both with side valves. A class win was managed in the Scottish Reliability Trials, but in August the company ran out of money.

Fifteen hundred employees were laid off and the company went into liquidation, but production continued, albeit reduced. With its assets written down, another new company, Argylls Limited, was set up under the control of Colonel J. S. Matthew of Dunlop's Scottish company, and at first it looked as though they would succeed. Fifty taxis had been exported to the United States for operation on the streets of New York and the new 12 horsepower model was finding public favour.

Alex Davidson joined the company as works manager from MMC and M. Perrot came from Brasier (France) as chief designer. The 1910 range reflected these personnel changes with a 10 horsepower twin costing £275, the 12/14 model at £285, a new 15 horsepower costing another £65, the 14/16 continuing at £375, a Twenty designed by Perrot at £445 and the company's first six-cylinder 30 horsepower model, which claimed 60 mph (97 km/h) and cost £525.

The Govan gearbox was replaced on all three new models by a gate-change type. A degree of rationalisation for 1911 dictated interchangeability of a large number of parts between all models, but the range was still too large. Only the 10, 20 and 30 horsepower models were continued for 1911, supplemented by a new Twelve with four-speed gearbox and, importantly, four-wheel brakes designed by Captain J. M. Rubury of Argyll's London depot.

Argyle Motor Manufacturing Company Limited of East Kilbride, Lanarkshire, built a few 16 ton 'Christina' trucks between 1970 and 1973 and even considered taking over the old Argyll (note the different spelling) works at Alexandria by Glasgow. Assembled from bought-in parts, the Argyle relied on Perkins diesel engines and other proprietary components.

Production was up from 240 cars in 1909 to 452 cars in 1910, but Alexandria could pay only if annual production exceeded a thousand vehicles. Argyll considered the double-sleeve Knight engine, but it was the simpler single-sleeve valve Burt-McCollum type which they eventually adopted in 1912, and a tuned 15/30 Argyll manned by Scott and Hornsted took 26 Class D records at Brooklands in 1913 including fourteen hours at 72.59 mph (117 km/h). A new range of cars fitted with the Burt-McCollum engine — the 15/30 and a 25/50 — were well made, attractive and technically interesting. Only the 12/18 with poppet valves lasted into 1914.

Charles Yale Knight's interests saw the Burt-McCollum engine as an infringement of their patent and sued Argyll. Argyll won their case but lost £50,000 defending the action and this, in addition to the fact that Alexandria cost £12,000 a month to run and had never paid since it was built, led to a liquidation meeting on 17th June 1914. In October 1915 John Brimlow took over the old Bridgeton works, but it is doubtful if more than three hundred Argylls made after the First World War found customers. Many of the components were 'bought out', including axles and engines from Greenwood and Batley of Leeds.

The revived 15/30 was joined by a Twelve in 1922 and in 1926 there appeared a sports 12/40 with front-wheel brakes. Brimlow showed Argylls at Olympia up to and including 1927, when a six-cylinder 18/50 model was announced but apparently never appeared, and after 1928 Bridgeton was merely a service depot for existing Argyll cars, finally closing in 1932.

The Argyll name still survives on a Scottish-built car, the Argyll Turbo GT. Built at Lochgilphead, Argyll (although the company moved to Lanark in 1988), and launched in 1983 by the Duke of Argyll, the car is a mid-engined 2 + 2 with 2.7 litre V6 engine and a turbo-charger system developed by Minnow Fish carburettors. It is aimed at the American market and carries coachwork by Avon of Warwick. Argyll cars have been in production since 1976, earlier versions being Saab or Rover V8-powered.

Craigton Engineering Works of Glasgow, operated by Angus Murray and Sons, produced about a dozen Atholl cars between 1907 and 1908. Of sturdy construction and fitted with a 25 horsepower engine, their main distinguishing feature was a radiator shaped like a Scottish bluebell.

OTHER SCOTTISH MOTOR MANUFACTURERS

AJR (1925-6): A. J. Robertson, 65 Queen Street, Edinburgh. Robertson was a popular designer/rider in motorcycle competition. His machines used JAP engines.

Alex (1908): Alexander and Company, Edinburgh. 14/18 horsepower model with four-cylinder Gnome engine and Rubery Owen chassis. Only one made.

All-British (1906-8): All-British Car Company, Bridgeton, Glasgow. Founded by George Johnston (late of Arrol-Johnston). Large complex car with horizontal eight-cylinder engine. Fewer than twelve sold.

Argyle (1970-3): Argyle Diesel Electronics Limited (later Argyle Motor Manufacturing Company Limited), East Kilbride, Lanarkshire. Christina truck with Perkins six-cylinder diesel engine, Eaton Yale and Towne five-speed gearbox and two-speed axle; cab by Motor Panels.

Argyll (1976 to date): Argyll Turbo Cars Limited, Minnow House, Lochgilphead, Argyll (later at Lanark). 150 mph (240 km/h) glass-fibre sports coupé with Triumph 2500 suspension and choice of turbo-charged Saab or Rover V-8 engines with five-speed ZF gearbox, later replaced by 2.7 litre V-6. Quality finish and trim by Avon Coachworks of Warwick.

Atholl (1907-8): Angus Murray and Sons, Craigton Engineering Works, Glasgow. A dozen 25 horsepower cars were built, with radiator shaped like a Scottish bluebell.

Beardmore (1919-28): Beardmore Motors Limited, Glasgow, Paisley (Renfrewshire) and Coatbridge (Lanarkshire). Largest of the minor manufacturers. Commenced with three models in three different factories, the Eleven, the Fifteen (mainly taxis) and the 4 litre Thirty. Well made, heavy and expensive cars, some with overhead camshafts. Taxis later built in London until 1967.

Beardmore (1936-7): William Beardmore and Company Limited, Dalmuir, Dunbartonshire. Oil-engined heavy trucks from 8 to 15 tons and single-

Beardmore maintained three separate factories in Glasgow, Paisley and Coatbridge, each producing a different model. This 1923 12/30 model was made in Glasgow, had sporting lines and useful performance and enjoyed some popularity. Note the forward-tilted radiator cap, a Beardmore trademark.

and double-decker buses, all with Beardmore's own engines.

Belhaven (1906-24): Robert Morton and Sons Limited (later Belhaven Engineering and Motors Limited), Wishaw, Lanarkshire. Initially steam wagons. Aster-engined petrol cabs built in Allanton foundry from 1908, then petrol-engined trucks and buses. Built Unitas trucks for United Co-operative Baking Society.

Bon-Car (1905-7): Edinburgh and Leith Engineering Company, Pirie Street, Leith, Edinburgh. Limited-production steam car, also known as the Bonne-Car.

Caledon (1915-27): Scottish Commercial Cars Limited (later Caledon Motors Limited), 94 Duke Street, Glasgow. Later renamed Scottish Commercial Cars and, in 1927, Richard Garrett and Company Limited. Used the cross of St Andrew as a radiator badge. Four hundred trucks built for the Army in the First World War by former Argyll employees Harry and Edward Tainsh. Initially four-tonners with Dorman engines and shaft or chain drive. Range extended from 30 cwt (1524 kg) to seven-tonners with Burt-McCollum single-sleeve valve engines. Meadows engines also tried. A rigid six-wheeler appeared in 1924 and a ten-tonner was catalogued in

1925. Taken over by steam engineers Richard Garrett and Company, of Leiston, Suffolk, who built just three Caledons.

Caledonian (1899-1906): Caledonian Motor Car and Cycle Company, 265 Union Street, Aberdeen. De Dion-engined voiturettes and larger Daimler-engined cars built to order only.

Caledonian (1910-11): Caledonia Motor Construction Company Limited, Granton Harbour, Edinburgh. Small producer of taxicabs.

Carlaw (1920): Carlaw Cars Limited, Glasgow. Austin agents who built three small commercials then sold the design to Harper Bean of Tipton, West Midlands, to become Bean 25 cwt (1270 kg) model.

Central (1900-3): Central Motor Company, 111 Bothwell Street, Glasgow. Mainly Aster and De Dion-engined cars. Four models from 6½ to 24 horsepower with twin- and four-cylinder engines.

Clyde (1913-32): McKay and Jardine, Main Street, Wishaw, Lanarkshire. Ex-employees of Belhaven producing trucks and buses initially with Aster engines, later with American Buda units. Made their own transmissions. Popular with Scottish bus operators.

Cotton (1909-11): Rennie and Prosser, 93-5 Mitchell Street, Glasgow. De-

Shaft-driven Caledon trucks gave endless trouble and the chain-driven version, seen here on the solid-tyred B Type, was more reliable. This example was operated by Herbert Brothers, bonded carmen of Millwall, London. Caledon had a strong following in London because of the efforts of their Swedish London sales manager, Mr Rinman.

Rennie and Prosser of Glasgow built at least seven, and possibly fifteen, Cotton motor cars for the Australian outback. With a 15 inch (380 mm) ground clearance and a fitted winch for pulling the car out of soft ground, the Cotton was also advertised as being capable of lifting weights and driving farm machinery. At least two survive in Australia.

BRITISH BUILT.

COTTON Motor Cars.

Specially constructed for Australian Bush requirements

to instructions of

A. J. COTTON, Esq.

THE ONLY PRACTICAL MOTOR CAR FOR A PRACTICAL BUSHMAN.

Sam Gilchrist, previously an engineer with the makers of the Caledon truck, commenced manufacture of the Gilchrist car in 1920. An 11.9 horsepower overhead-valve version of the Hotchkiss engine used in the Bullnose Morris powered the car, which had an aluminium radiator and bodywork by Sims and Wilson of Cathcart, Glasgow.

This 30 cwt (1524 kg) Halley of about 1910 is typical of the firm's products during their heyday before the First World War, when they probably outsold their nearest rivals, Albion. This delivery van probably has the 38/32 model four-cylinder engine, but a 16 horsepower twin was also available.

signed by A. J. Cotton specifically for the Australian outback. 24 horsepower White and Poppe engine, 15 inch (380 mm) ground clearance and built-in winch. About fifteen built.

Dalgleish-Gullane (1907-8): Haddington Motor Engineering Company, Haddington, East Lothian. De Dion-engined 8 horsepower light car with shaft drive. Only ten built.

Dalhousie (1906-10): Anderson-Grice Company Limited, Carnoustie, Angus. Designed by A. G. Grice (later of GWK), four-cylinder cars with steeply raked radiators and racy lines. James Law of Arbroath took over in 1910.

DL (1913-20): W. Guthrie and Company, Motherwell, Lanarkshire (later DL Motor Manufacturing Company Limited). 8 and 10/12 horsepower cars and light commercials with V-radiators and four-cylinder engines. Taken over by Wallace (Glasgow) Limited in 1920.

Drummond (1905-9): North British Manufacturing Company Limited, Dumfries. Based on 20/24 horsepower Special built by D. McKay Drummond of Dumfries Ironworks for use in trials. Several 20/24 and 14/16 horsepower cars built. Also known as North-British.

Dunalistair (1925-6): Dunalistair Cars Limited, 194 Birkin Avenue, Nottingham (later 22 West Regent Street, Glasgow). 14 horsepower Meadows-engined car with chassis by Mechins of Glasgow. Used the cross of St Andrew as radiator badge. Only four built.

Dunedin (*c*.1912): George E. Rutherford, Cycle Maker, Edinburgh. Assembled JAP-engined machines called after the ancient name for Edinburgh.

Ferox (1914): Ferox Light Car Company, Paisley, Renfrewshire. Ballot-engined 1.3 litre four-cylinder light car with shaft drive. Very few built.

Fraser (1911): Douglas Fraser and Sons, Arbroath, Angus. Three- and four-cylinder steam cars with single-acting poppet-valve engines and coil-tube boiler.

Gilchrist (1920-3): Sam Gilchrist, Orchard Drive, Giffnock, Glasgow (later Gilchrist Cars Limited, Govan, Glasgow). Built by ex-Caledon employee. 12 horsepower overhead-valve Hotchkiss-engined car, bodied by Sims and Wilson of Cathcart, Glasgow. About twenty built.

Glasgow (1920): Wallace (Glasgow) Limited, Cardonald, Glasgow. Three-wheeled agricultural tractor with drive to all three wheels and Burt-McCollum single-sleeve valve engine. Taken over by British Motor Trading Corporation Limited.

Grampian (1908): Grampian Engineering and Motor Company, Stirling. A few steam- and petrol-engined lorries were built.

Granton (1905-7): Scottish Motor Engineering Company, Granton Harbour, Edinburgh. Twin-cylinder trucks and a 40 horsepower chain-driven bus built in small numbers.

GRI (1921-2): Macrae and Dick, Inverness. Designed by G. R. Inshaw, an interesting motorcycle in which a four-stroke engine was used but a single valve did duty for both inlet and exhaust.

Halley (1901-35): Glasgow Motor Lorry Company Limited, Finnieston Street, Glasgow (later Crownpoint Road, Glasgow); then Halley's Industrial Motors Limited, Yoker, Glasgow. Second in importance as commercial vehicle builders only to Albion, Halley was a major supplier outside Scotland for fifteen years. It was founded by George Halley. Initially Glasgow steam trucks were built but were superseded by petrol-engined types. Up to the First World War, a wide range from 1 ton to 6 tons capacity was produced, including passenger vehicles for from ten to forty people. Tylor engines were used for heavy trucks, but from 1911 Halley built its own engines at Linwood. Fire engines and other municipal vehicles became a speciality. Four hundred vehicles were supplied to the Army during the First World War, thereafter concentrating on 3½ tonners with (perhaps uniquely) six-cylinder engines. Financial problems dogged the company, particularly after Halley's death in 1921. In 1934 the company belatedly introduced the Perkins Leopard diesel engine but was liquidated in September 1935. Albion took over the works but sold all the spares and undertook no production under the Halley name.

Harper (1898-1900, 1905-6, 1908): Harper Motor Company, Holburn Junction, Aberdeen. Initially crude tractor-type vehicles with Benz or Cannstatt-Daimler engines. Petrol cars based on single-cylinder Cadillac built 1905/6. A few steam trucks in 1908.

JP (1950-4): Joseph Potts Limited, Bellshill, Lanarkshire. Some 33 racing cars built, the first based on a Cooper 500 Formula type with tubular frame and De Dion-type rear axle.

Kelvin (1904-6): Bergius Car and Engine Company, Finnieston Street, Glasgow. Some fourteen 14 horsepower four-cylinder cars were built with rear-entrance tonneau bodywork. Then production began of marine engines, for which the firm is still famous.

Kennedy (1907-10): Hugh Kennedy and Company, Glasgow. A few 15/20 horsepower four-cylinder cars built, also known as Ailsa.

Kingsburgh (1901-2): Kingsburgh Motor Construction Company, Granton, Edinburgh. Successors to the Madelvic. 12 horsepower cars and motor buses made.

Lothian (1913-24): Scottish Motor Traction Company Limited, Edinburgh. Designed by W. J. Thompson, buses with Belgian-built Minerva Silent Knight sleeve-valve engine, and worm-drive by David Brown of Huddersfield, West Yorkshire. For SMT use only. From 1914 Tylor-engined 3 ton truck offered to other operators. 97 built. SMT later assembled Bethlehem and Reo trucks and buses.

Madelvic (1898-1900): Madelvic Carriage Company Limited, Granton, Edinburgh. Founded by William Peck, Astronomer Royal for Scotland. Electric broughams with front-wheel-drive power unit, also used to convert horse-drawn carriages.

Mearns (1899-1902): John Tavendale, Millwright and Cyclemaker, Laurencekirk, Kincardineshire. Cars initially powered by engines cast by Endurance Motor Company of Coventry, West Midlands, later renamed 'St Laurence' and fitted with 6 horsepower Accles and Turrell engines and dogcart bodywork.

Milton (1920-1): Belford Motor Company, Edinburgh. Friction-driven 9 and 10 horsepower cars powered by Alpha, Decolange or Dorman engines. Transverse-leaf front suspension. Body hinged upwards to facilitate servicing.

Neale (1897): Douglas Neale, Edinburgh. High, electric-powered dogcarts bodied by Drew of Edinburgh, driven by one rear wheel only. Only four built.

New Gerard (1922-36): New Gerard Motors, Gayfield Square, Edinburgh (later 27 Greenside Place, Edinburgh). Blackburne or JAP-engined motorcycles designed by J. A. 'Jock' Porter. Won the 1923 Lightweight and 1924 Ultra Lightweight TT. Between 1924 and 1927 built in Campion factory, Nottingham.

Overdale (1921-2): Glasgow. Obscure 269 cc Villiers-engined motorcycle.

Probe (1971): Caledonian Probe Motor Company, Irvine, Ayrshire (1969-71 at Bradford-on-Avon, Wiltshire). Futuristic cars designed by Dennis Adams (ex-Marcos), with rear-mounted British Leyland 1800 engines. About twelve built.

This Kelvin car of about 1906 is one of the last of only fourteen built and was owned by A. C. Denny of Dumbarton. A 16 horsepower example, it carries the distinctive high-backed body favoured by its makers and has the refinement of a windscreen. It is registered SN 99, a Dunbartonshire issue.

The larger 11.9 horsepower Rob Roy, built at Hugh Kennedy's Koh-i-noor Works at Shettleston, Glasgow, employed a conventional four-cylinder engine by Dorman's of Stafford. A 10 horsepower model with Coventry-Climax engine was also offered in 1923/4 but by 1925 the company was in liquidation.

Renfrew (1904): Scottish Motor Carriage Company, Glasgow. 16/20 horsepower car costing £400. Took part in Scottish Automobile Club Trials, 1904.

Ridley (1901-7): Ridley Autocar Company, Coventry, West Midlands (later Ridley Motor Company Limited, George Place, Paisley, Renfrewshire). Early experiments with Horbick chassis fitted with engines designed by John Ridley followed the failure of his Coventry venture. Few cars sold after 1906 from Paisley.

Robertson (1900-2): William Robertson and Sons, Bell Street, Dundee. Obscure makers of tricycles, voiturettes and cars.

Robertson (1934): J. W. Robertson, Drymen, Stirlingshire. Low-slung sports car with V-4 single-sleeve valve two-stroke engine with twin-diameter pistons and sleeves. Maximum speed 65 mph (105 km/h). Later named Cowal.

Rob Roy (1922-6): Kennedy Motor Company Limited, Koh-i-noor Works, Shettleston, Glasgow. Cyclecar with own flat-twin engine (also supplied to Kingsbury Junior of London). Later light cars with 10 and 12 horsepower engines by Coventry-Climax and Dorman. Named after Sir Walter Scott's hero.

Royal Scot (1922-4): Donaldson and Kelso (later Knightswood Motors Limited), Strathcona Drive, Anniesland, Glasgow (later 98 West George Street, Glasgow). All-Scottish motorcycle with frames by Victoria and sleeve-valve Barr and Stroud engines.

Scotia (c.1907): Springfield Road, Bridgeton, Glasgow. Ephemeral 16/20 horsepower four-cylinder car, possibly also offered as a commercial.

Scotsman (1922-3): Scotsman Motor Car Company, Wigton Street, Glasgow. 10 and 11 horsepower cars. Later 14/40 Flying Scotsman model with overhead-camshaft Sage engine. Radiator shaped like Scottish thistle.

Scotsman (1929-30): Scotsman Motors Limited, Gorgie, Edinburgh. Six-cylinder air-cooled car based on French SARA. Later 11.9 horsepower Meadows-engined model known as Little Scotsman.

Seetstu (1906-7): James McGeoch and Company, 11 Incle Street, Paisley, Renfrewshire. Six or seven light two-seaters with three wheels and 3 horsepower two-stroke engine.

Sentinel (1906-17, then at Shrewsbury, Shropshire, until 1956): Alley and McLellan Limited, Polmadie, Glasgow. Well engineered steam lorries. Early models with vertical boilers by

29

Right: *Before
their move to
Shrewsbury in
1917, Sentinel
steam wagons
were built by
Alley and
McLellan Li-
mited of Pol-
madie, Glas-
gow. This 6
ton Standard
Sentinel was
capable of
hauling 10
tons (with a
trailer).*

*Left: The second car to bear the Scotsman
name (the first was built in Glasgow and partly
financed by Sir Harry Lauder) was made in
1930 in Gorgie, Edinburgh, based on the
French air-cooled SARA. Some thirty to forty
cars were sold. Later, more conventional!
models, like this one, were fitted with 11.9
horsepower water-cooled Meadows engines
and known as the Little Scotsman.*

Skeogh (1921): J. B. Skeogh, Burnside
Motor Works, Dalbeattie, Kirkcud-
brightshire. Ten chain-drive cyclecars
built with 348 cc Precision engines.
Fire destroyed the factory.

Stewart-Thornycroft (1902 to c.1910):
Duncan Stewart and Company (1902)
Limited, London Road Ironworks,
Glasgow. Fixed and marine engine
builders whose vehicle production
centred on Thornycroft types built
under licence. These locomotive-
boilered radial valve-gear types were
followed by Stewart's own Colonial
models from 1907.

Stirling (1897-1907): J. and C. Stirling,
Hamilton, Lanarkshire (later Stirling's
Motor Carriages Limited, and from
1902 at Granton, Edinburgh). Early
vehicles based on Daimler chassis and
engines, but with own bodywork. Im-
ported Clement-Panhards sold as
Stirling-Panhard or Clement-Stirling.
From 1902 concentrated on lorries and
buses.

Abbot and Company of Newark, Not-
tinghamshire, cross water tubes and
superheaters. Mainly five-tonners,
continued in Shrewsbury until 1923
when Super Sentinel introduced.
Some overtypes sold in 1911.

Simpson (1897-1904): John Simpson,
Whins of Milton, Stirling. Some
twenty steam cars built with 6, 10 or 12
horsepower engines. Early dogcarts
with double suspension (chassis
sprung on axles, body sprung on
chassis).

St Vincent (1903-10): William McLean (later St Vincent Motor and Cycle Company Limited), 161-9 North Street, Glasgow. Cars and commercials from 12 to 40 horsepower with Aster engines and chassis. Later called 'Scottish Aster'. Some taxicabs after 1910.

Tod (1897): Michael Tod and Sons, Dunfermline, Fife. Primitive, experimental three-wheeler with four-cylinder engine. Only one built.

Victoria (1906-7): Victoria (Peacock) and Autocar Company, Craigpark Works, Dennistoun, Glasgow. Modified Chenard-Walckers and Peugeots rebuilt and sold as Victorias.

Victoria (1902-26): Victoria Motor and Cycle Company Limited, Dennistoun, Glasgow. Largest Scottish motorcycle works. Used Villiers, JAP, Blackburne, Coventry-Victor, Precision and their own engines.

Waverley (1901-4): Scottish Motor Company, Leith Walk, Edinburgh (later New Rossleigh Motor and Cycle Company Limited, Hope Crescent, Edinburgh). 'Pride of the North', a 9 horsepower De Dion Bouton-engined light car with three speeds.

Werbell (1907-9): W. and E. Raikes-Bell, Dundee. White and Poppe-engined 25 horsepower cars. Only about eight built. Name taken from initials of builders, William and Edward Raikes-Bell.

WSC (1914): Wholesale Supply Company, Aberdeen. Friction-driven cyclecar built by the Co-op. 8 horsepower JAP V-twin engine and belt final drive.

The diminutive Skeogh was one of very few makes of cyclecar to have been built in Scotland. Exhibited at the 1921 Kelvin Hall Show, and built by J. B. Skeogh (previously an employee of Belhaven) at Burnside Motor Works, Dalbeattie, only eight or ten were sold before fire destroyed the works.

A St Vincent opendrive three-quarter landaulette of 1906. The company built its own coachwork to the high standard of the day, but virtually all the mechanical components and chassis were supplied by Aster of Wembley.

FURTHER READING

Baldwin, N. 'Caledon', *Old Motor Magazine*, July/August 1973.
Baldwin, N. 'Halley', *Old Motor Magazine*, volume 10, numbers 5 and 6.
Browning, A. S. E. *Scottish Cars*. Glasgow Art Gallery and Museum, 1962.
Doyle, G. R. *The World's Automobiles*. Temple Press, fourth edition 1963.
Georgano, G. N. *The Complete Encyclopaedia of Commercial Vehicles*. Krause Publications, 1979.
Georgano, G. N. *A History of the London Taxicab*. David and Charles, 1972.
Georgano, G. N. *The World's Commercial Vehicles*. Temple Press, 1963.
Georgano, G. N. *The Complete Encyclopaedia of Motor Cars*. Ebury Press, 1968.
Hunter, D. G. L. *Scottish Buses before 1928*. Turntable Enterprises, 1973.
Jarman, L. 'Gilchrist', *Old Motor Magazine*, January 1963.
Lambie, B. *Thomas Blackwood Murray*. Gladstone Court Museum, 1971.
Macdonald, A. Craig, and Browning, A. S. E. *History of the Motor Industry in Scotland*. Institution of Automobile Engineers, 1960.
Montagu of Beaulieu, Lord. *Lost Causes of Motoring*. Cassell, 1966.
Robertson, D. *Scotland's Motoring Story*. McKenzie Vincent, 1960.
Tragatsch, E. *The World's Motorcycles 1894-1963*. Temple Press, 1964.
Tragatsch, E. *The Illustrated Encyclopaedia of Motorcycles*. Temple Press, 1983.
Worthington-Williams, M. 'Cars from Scotland', *The Scots Magazine*, March 1975.

PLACES TO VISIT

Although a number of Scottish-manufactured vehicles are preserved in private ownership (about sixty survive in all) there are not many in museums. The following are exceptions.

Braidwood and Rushbrook Fire Museum, McDonald Road, Edinburgh EH3 9DE. Telephone: 031-228 2401. Example of a 1910 Halley 75 horsepower six-cylinder engine fire engine.

Doune Motor Museum, Carse of Cambus, Doune, Perthshire. Telephone: 0786 841203. Example of Arrol-Johnston.

Gladstone Court, Biggar, Lanarkshire ML12 6DT. Telephone: 0899 21050. The reference library includes the Albion factory records.

Glasgow Museum of Transport, Kelvin Hall, Bunhouse Road, Glasgow G3 8PZ. Telephone: 041-357 3929. Examples of Arrol-Johnston, Argyll and Albion are included.

Grampian Transport Museum, Alford, Aberdeenshire AB3 8AD. Telephone: 0336 2292. Includes the Craigievar Express, a steam tricycle built by a local postman in 1895.

Myreton Motor Museum, Aberlady, East Lothian. Telephone: 08757 288. Examples of Galloway, Arrol-Aster and Arrol-Johnston.

National Motor Museum, John Montagu Building, Beaulieu, Brockenhurst, Hampshire SO4 7ZN. Telephone: 0590 612345. Excellent reference library and examples of Argyll, Albion and Hillman Imp.

Royal Museum of Scotland, Chambers Street, Edinburgh EH1 1JF. Telephone: 031-225 7534.

Science Museum, Exhibition Road, South Kensington, London SW7 2DD. Telephone: 01-938 8000. Albion lorry at Wroughton and Beardmore aero-engine at South Kensington.